T0003202

THE YOUNG INFLUENCER'S HANDBOOK

The Young Influencer's Handbook:
Build Your Brand, Gain Followers, Secure Sponsorships, and Create Click-worthy Content

13-Digit ISBN: 978-1-64643-165-6
10-Digit ISBN: 1-64643-165-0

This book may be ordered by mail from the publisher. Please include $5.99 for postage and handling. Please support your local bookseller first!

Books published by Cider Mill Press Book Publishers are available at special discounts for bulk purchases in the United States by corporations, institutions, and other organizations. For more information, please contact the publisher.

Applesauce Press is an imprint of
Cider Mill Press Book Publishers
"Where good books are ready for press"
PO Box 454
12 Spring Street
Kennebunkport, Maine 04046

Visit us online! cidermillpress.com

Typography: Brandon Grotesque, Neutraface 2 Display

Printed in China

1 2 3 4 5 6 7 8 9 0

First Edition

THE YOUNG INFLUENCER'S HANDBOOK

BUILD YOUR BRAND, GAIN FOLLOWERS, SECURE SPONSORSHIPS, AND CREATE CLICK-WORTHY CONTENT

KENNEBUNKPORT, MAINE

TABLE OF CONTENTS

Introduction 7

The Influencer Lifestyle 8

Mastering the Platforms: TikTok,
Instagram, YouTube, and Twitter 22

Building Your Brand 50

Themes & Visual Style 64

Gaining Followers 70

Know Your Audience 84

Perfecting Your Content: Caption Writing,
Video Editing, and Photo Tips 90

The Art of the Hashtag 102

Digital Marketing 108

How to Stand Out from the Crowd 116

Working with Brands and Getting Sponsors 122

Monetizing Your Platform & Negotiating Your Worth 128

Final Thoughts 140

INTRODUCTION

What is an influencer? A lot of people say they are influencers, and a lot of people wish they were. But sometimes, people who say they are influencers aren't really, or they aren't as influential as they think they are! Others say nothing about themselves, but have huge followings, with people hanging on their every word. They might be an "influencer" on just about any topic: clothing and fashion, books, video games, food, movies or TV, music, lifestyles, you name it; somewhere, somebody is influencing somebody else!

This book will talk about what an influencer is, what they do, who they reach out to, and how you can become one. With social media being such a huge part of everyone's lives these days, it's easier than ever to get noticed online for being the special person you are. It doesn't even cost much (or any) money, if you do it right. But it's also that much harder to get recognized now, because anyone can do it. So how can you get in on it all and stand out? How can you influence people, their buying choices, and their lives in a positive way? This little book will give you some great tips and advice to get going!

THE INFLUENCER LIFESTYLE

So what is an influencer?

- Basically, an influencer is someone who has built a reputation for knowledge and expertise on a topic, and uses their online presence to "influence" their followers on things like purchasing and lifestyle choices.

- Influencers often partner with businesses and bigger companies who want their names/faces attached to products, to make them easier to sell.

Influencers build a genuine relationship with their followers in a way that ordinary advertising doesn't.

Influencers are people first, not businesses, though they might well have businesses of their own.

- An influencer has a following of their own. This is a large number of people in a specific niche or area, people that "get" what the influencer is saying and offering.

- Influencers build a genuine relationship with their followers in a way that ordinary advertising doesn't. They post to their social media profiles regularly and encourage follower comments and engagement.

- Influencers are people first, not businesses, though they might well have businesses of their own.

That all sounds good, but you might but wondering if there different types of influencers? The answer is yes! Here are some of the most common types (note: not everyone uses these names):

- **Mega influencers:** These are the big celebrities, the Kardashians, the movie stars, the pop stars, athletes, and so on. These people can have millions of followers, and their endorsement of a product gives it total credibility. Every other influencer probably wants to be one of these folks!

- **Macro influencers:** This is the next step down from the big stars. These might by actors who are famous, but not leads, or it might be musicians that are popular, but not gold-selling stars. They might also be best-selling authors or tech or business people who have a great reputation in their fields. They usually have at least tens of thousands of followers, sometimes a lot more.

- **Micro influencers:** these are the "normal" people who have developed a following because of their expertise on a topic. They likely started very small and grew organically. This is probably where a lot of the people you think of as "influencers" actually hang out. They may have a few thousand followers, or tens of thousands.

- **Nano influencers:** These are the babies, the ones just starting out. These influencers may have a lot of knowledge about a very narrow subject, but that's not a bad thing. They may have 1,000 followers or less. If you're just beginning, you're probably here.

Okay, that's all good! So how do you become one? Well, there are several things you'll have to do to get started:

- **Choose your niche/subject.** In order to be an influencer, you have to know who you're going to influence and what you're going to be influencing them about. What is the thing you love talking about? What is the subject you know so much about that you can't wait to tell others about every new story or development? That's your niche.

What is the thing you love talking about? What is the subject you know so much about that you can't wait to tell others about every new story or development? That's your niche.

- **What social media platforms do you want to use?** You can't be an influencer with social media profiles. You're probably already on several of them, but pick your favorite one or two, at most, when you start out; you need to focus your attention on that small space at the beginning. The point is to get followers, and to do that, you need to be in a limited number of places.

- **Consider creating a business profile/account.** You probably already have a personal page or two, but it's a good idea to make your new social media presence a business one. You'll get extra tools for advertising and marketing, and the cred of having a "professional" page!

Don't hesitate to talk to friends and see what they would like, or ask the advice of a professional.

- **Create a good look and design for your page.** You want to be inviting and to have people come to you, so put up your best profile photo, and try to create a look that will express what you want. If you're having trouble with this, look at what other influencers are doing to get some ideas. Don't hesitate to talk to friends and see what they would like, or ask the advice of a professional designer.

- **Think about the followers you want.** We'll get into this more below, but it's important that you consider who you want as followers. You won't attract everyone, so you need to have an idea of who you do want.

- **Post things that your followers will like.** It seems silly to say, but this is the most important part, and it's why you need to understand who's following you. You need to create new content pretty much

It's important that you consider who you want as followers. You won't attract everyone, so you need to have an idea of who you do want.

constantly, especially at the start. Yes, this can be exhausting, but it's essential if your name and reputation are going to grow. If you can't post every day, try to post every other day, or at least three times a week; you just have to!

- **Be sure to engage with your followers.** You're not just there, putting on a show. People will comment on your posts, and it's necessary to respond, engage, chat, etc. It's a way to develop a connection to your followers. If they know that you're not distant from them, they'll be more likely to comment, hoping to hear back from you. Of course, as you get more popular, you won't be able to respond to everyone, but that's a good problem to have!

- **Pay attention to what others are saying and who contacts you.** If you start getting better known, you may be approached by other influencers and even businesses about partnering up (see below). Do it! This is a great way to grow your online presence even more.

- **Don't take negative comments personally.** Sure, that's easy to say! At some point, someone will say something unkind, or just downright mean or rude to you, or about you. You can't please everybody, and you have to be okay with that. Of course if someone is harassing you, then definitely report them and block them. But just know that with fame comes the jerks who want to ruin your day. Don't let them.

At some point, someone will say something unkind, or just downright mean or rude to you, or about you. You can't please everybody, and you have to be okay with that.

MASTERING THE PLATFORMS: TIKTOK, INSTAGRAM, YOUTUBE, AND TWITTER

Okay, so you've decided to be an influencer, and you know you need to be on social media. But which platforms/sites are the right ones for you?

Social media is not only your friend, it's completely necessary to do any kind of real influencing! Only you can decide which platform(s) are best for you. You probably don't need to be on all of them, unless you really want to; it can get confusing and even exhausting trying to keep up! So how do you decide? Ask yourself these questions:

- Which platforms are most comfortable to you?

- Which platforms do you know best?

- Which platforms are the ones you like the most?

- Which platforms are most likely to have the kinds of people on them that you want as followers?

- Which platforms can you keep up with and post to every day?

With those questions in mind, here are some things to know about some of the most popular social media sites, as well as what you should and shouldn't do on them. Also, remember that new social media sites seem to be appearing all the time, and it's a good idea to keep a watch for what's trending, and what's going to be the next big thing.

TikTok

TikTok is, by design, different from many other social media platforms. It became very popular in 2020, as millions were stuck inside from the COVID pandemic and were looking for new online entertainment and content to pass the time. Like every social media site, TikTok has its own particular rules.

- **Look at the trends.** Trends are very important on TikTok. Try to keep up and see which ones

Remember that new social media sites seem to be appearing all the time, and it's a good idea to keep a watch for what's trending.

might match your area of influence, and use those hashtags when you post. Try checking trending audio as well, to see what songs are trending.

- **Use duets when you can.** Duets let you place your own video alongside another, and even stack several of them in a row (think of the sea shanty song that took the internet by storm in early 2021!). The other poster has to have duets enabled, of course, or you won't be able to do it. But if you can work out an idea with another influencer, duets can be funny and great fun!

- **Try to be creative with your videos.** Users want new things. It can be difficult to come up with new ideas all the time, of course, but don't just rely on the same idea for every video.

- **Make sure your posts have value.** They should be about your presence. What are you offering to others?

- **Use your videos to teach.** TikTok users love to learn new things, so if you can post a video that shows them something new related to your area of influence, you're going to get a better response. Think tutorials, advice, helpful hints, etc.

- **Share your videos on other sites.** TikTok prioritizes these posts, because you're giving the site free advertising, so make sure to share you post directly from the app to Twitter, Instagram, or even Facebook.

- **Remember, your videos are short, so make the most of them.** This isn't YouTube, and you're limited in time.

- **Try using multiple angles of yourself.** This takes a little more work, but if you change camera angles, it gives your video variety and makes it more interesting. You don't have to be a world-class cinematographer, just try getting creative with shooting yourself from different angles. Maybe try different times and different outfits for fun.

- **Use effects and filters, but not too much.** They can make your video stand out, but if you overdo it, you may look tacky and cheesy. This is especially true of Bling! Not everything needs to sparkle. Be careful.

- **Comment on your videos.** People like a bit of context. Do things that are relevant to your followers, like asking them a question that they can answer in the comments. Use only a few hashtags, and make them count by making them unique. Include your Instagram handle, as well: "IG: @ yourusername"

You don't have to be a world-class cinematographer, just try getting creative.

- **Try to post twice a day, if you can.** This might be more work than you can handle when you start, but the more you can post, the greater your chances of being seen.

Twitter

Twitter is a funny beast. Sometimes, it can feel like shouting at a brick wall, if nothing you post gets any reactions! It can be frustrating, but it's also a great place to try to interact with famous people of all kinds. Here are some ideas to make the most of it:

- **Pick the right photos for your main page.** You want them to represent you and what your message is. It may not even be a picture of you, if you have a brand or a logo you'd rather have there. Make sure that a relevant link to your preferred website is also there.

- **Post several times a day.** Since tweets are short, it doesn't hurt, and can only help you to be a presence on Twitter as often as possible. Sure, it is possible to overdo it, but as long as you're not posting every ten minutes, people probably won't get too annoyed with you!

- **Make sure you're posting exactly what you want to say.** Twitter (still!) won't let you edit, so read it over before you post.

- **Tweets don't have to be long, even with the character limit.** Unless you have something really important to say, which is going to take several tweets, it's fine to keep them kind of short.

- **Be creative with your tweets.** Twitter is where you can have a bit more freedom to post things that aren't necessarily about you and your message or brand. Did you see a funny animal video? It's fine

Twitter is where you can have a bit more freedom to post things that aren't necessarily about you and your message or brand.

to retweet it, if you think it will make others smile and laugh, too. Of course, you should try to post about your area of influence, but don't be afraid to wander a bit. It might even bring in new followers. Not every tweet needs to be about you!

- **Try out fleets.** Fleets are a new-ish feature on Twitter, offering you to the chance to post short videos for a limited time; basically Twitter's answer to TikTok and other similar platforms. Use them in the same way.

- **Use hashtags, but not too much.** Two or three in a post is fine.

- **Engage with your followers.** As with other social media, take time to talk with people who comment on your posts. You want them to feel valued.

- **You don't have to follow everyone back who follows you.** Don't feel obligated. If they really like what you're doing, they'll follow you in any case. And if they unfollow you for not following them back, they weren't interested in you, anyway.

Instagram

Instagram has its own set of guidelines about how to get the most out of it. Here are some tips:

- **Post every day, if possible.** At least try to post several times a week. The best way to do this is to have a schedule and stick to it. Not only is this easier for you, your followers will know when to expect new content from you. So maybe you post each day at 11:00 am, and again at 4:00 pm, or maybe you do that every Monday, Wednesday, and Friday. You'll want to experiment and see which days and times get you the most likes and comments.

- **Be sure to put important info on your home page.** You only get one external link with Instagram, so make it count! You can change it as often as you like, so if you post something interesting that has a link, be sure to direct your followers back to it on your main page. Put a new link up every day, if that's what you need to do!

- **Post things that are relevant.** It can be fun to post whatever you want, but on Instagram, it's usually better to post content and images that are connected to your area of influence. Random cat pictures can be fun once in a while, but if they don't relate to what your followers want from you, you might lose them if you do too much off-topic posting.

- **Use hashtags!** Hashtags are your friends! Hashtags are essential on Instagram. Use them often, use a lot of them! Ten or twelve in one post is usually okay. The point is that you want others to see what you're posting, so make them relevant.

- **Post videos regularly.** It's been said that if you don't, your image posts will be shown to fewer of your followers. Yes, that doesn't seem fair, but that's how the site works (this is not official; it's just what some users have noticed). Your videos don't need to be long, but they need to go up often.

- **What if you have trouble thinking of new content?** Yes, you can run out of ideas. One of the best ways to fix this is simply to ask your followers what they want to see. It's a great way to get them involved and keep them entertained.

YouTube

YouTube takes a bit more thought, since you need to post more than minute-long videos to keep followers engaged. Well, it's okay to do that once in a while, but your regular posts should be a bit more meaningful than that. Here are some things to keep in mind if/when you start a YouTube channel:

- **Know why you're there.** Can you post videos with enough content to make it worth your time and other people's time? Just having a channel where you never post anything won't do you any good, and you won't attract any followers; no one wants to follow a channel that posts new videos twice a year! Basically, is YouTube right for you?

- **Make sure you have a decent video camera, sound, and background.** You don't have to be in a professional studio, but you need to make sure the video looks good, people can hear you, and that you're not surrounded by a dump! You don't need to spend a lot of money on this. Even using a clean bedroom as a background is fine.

- **Post often.** You don't need to post every day, unless you really want to, but at least once a week is a good idea. If your videos are longer, it's going to take some time to shoot and edit them, so take that into account when you decide how often you want to post. And don't post a video just to have something up. You need to be giving valuable content to your subscribers.

- **Be sure to post links and keywords.** Always let viewers know about where else they can find you online, and use the right keywords that match the content of your video so that it comes up in searches. If there are other influencers you like, give them a shout-out and link to their channels.

- **Partner with others.** People who follow various influencers love to see them get together. If you can do a team-up video with another influencer, it's likely your own people will love it! This can be a conversation, a Q&A, whatever you want. Reach out to your friends and see who's up for it!

- **Viral is overrated.** Sure, everyone wants a post or video to go viral, but it's pretty hard to control if that will happen, no matter what anyone says to you. You're better off giving your viewers good content and letting them spread the word about you. If you have a great video, word will get out.

- **Interact with your viewers when you can.** If they post nice things about you in the comments, take the time to thank them. If they ask questions, answer what you can. Of course, if you get popular and have tons of comments, you're not going to have the time to go through them all, but that's a good problem to have!

- **What about ads?** This is a tricky one. People hate when they pop up in the model of videos, but they do pay you, so you'll have to experiment and see what your followers will tolerate.

Snapchat

Obviously, Snapchat posts don't last long, so you'll need to make an impact while they're up! Here are some ways to make the most of the platform:

- **Post more than once a day.** Since your videos will be gone in twenty-four hours, you'll need to do a lot of them to really get noticed. This might be more work than you can commit to, so make sure you want to do it before committing to Snapchat.

Ask questions,
get opinions,
get posting.

- **Try creating a sponsored lens or filter.** See the website for details. These are fun and funny, and you'll make an impression if you can make people laugh.

- **Reach out to your followers to engage with you.** Ask questions, get their opinions, get them posting. If you're endorsing a product, get them to send in their own pictures of the product, too!

- **Make sure your stories stay short.** They're only up for twenty-four hours, anyway, so don't make them too long.

- **Stick to your brand.** Snapchat is not the place to post random stuff!

- **Don't add sound to every post.** People may look at your post on their phones with the sound off. If you use it every time, they'll be missing some of your content.

- **Have fun!** Snapchat posts don't have to be perfect; they just need to engage your followers.

Keep your eyes open for the latest social media platforms. New ones seem to be popping up all the time, and it's worth your time to try to get in early on some of them, if they feel right to you. But remember that it's always worth learning about security and safety of course, even with established sites. Be careful until enough people can confirm a new site isn't a scam.

It's always worth learning about security and safety.

Getting Known with Podcasts and Webinars

Podcasts and webinars can be a great way of getting your name out there, and positioning yourself as an expert and an influencer. The best part is, they cost very little, or nothing at all, but allow you to reach a lot of people. Don't overlook these two valuable tools!

Podcasts

Podcasts are everywhere! And they're for everyone! No matter what you do, what you're interested in, and what you want, there's a podcast out there for you. And that means that you, as an influencer, can find a nice market of people willing to listen to you, if they want to follow you. Right now, there are three main ways you can use podcasts, but only two will probably interest you.

- **You can advertise on podcasts that are already out there.** Unless you have a business that's selling something (like a product or a service), this probably won't be something you need to do. But if you do, maybe think about it. Advertising costs money, though, so keep that in mind.

- **You can be a guest on an existing podcast.** This is a great way to reach new listeners and get new followers. Is there a podcast that you love listening to that's all about the same things you like and want to influence? Reach out and see if you can go on as a guest. Even if you only get a few minutes to talk, it's a chance to get your name out there to others who have common interest. It's a built-in audience!

- **You can start your own podcast!** You can control exactly what you want to talk about, have guests that you want, and make it all for the people that already follow you. Make one a week, one a month,

No matter what you do, what you're interested in, and what you want, there's a podcast out there for you.

whatever works. And they don't have to be super long; in fact, it might be better to keep them short if you're just starting out. There are several companies that offer free podcast software, so see which one is right for you.

Webinars:

A webinar might seem like strange thing to want to do; aren't they usually for teaching and boring business stuff? Yes, they are, but what if you held one as an event for your followers to talk about something new and exciting that they'll be interested in? It's worth a try!

- **Make sure it's really offering your followers value. If you can do it on a YouTube video instead, then do it there.**

- **Make sure you're only talking about one thing.** Make it the big news and leave it at that, as long as it's enough content to justify a having webinar!

- **Don't make it too long. People might get pretty bored if it goes on for more than thirty minutes.** Would you want to sit through what you're talking about?

- **Use your webinar to mark yourself out as an influencer and expert.** Just like everything else you do, the point is to establish yourself as the influencer, so make sure you stay on topic.

- **Make time for questions at the end. It's a great way** to get your audience engaged and keep them interested! They get to talk to you in person, wow!

BUILDING YOUR BRAND

Being an influencer means having a recognizable brand and building it over time. A "brand" doesn't just mean something like a line of clothing or a tennis shoe. It can definitely be those things, but it can also be what people think of when they think of you. Your brand can be your message, your music, your face, even your reputation; whatever else you associate yourself with that makes you unique. So, you have to ask yourself some very important questions. Take time to think about these and how you'll answer them.

A "brand" is what people think of when they think of you.

Your brand can
be your message,
your music, your
face, even your
reputation;
whatever else you
associate yourself
with that makes
you unique.

- **Who are you?** You may know that, but most other people don't. And if you don't know that, start with asking yourself, "who am I?"

- **What's different about you?** What sets you apart from other influencers in your group? What makes you unique?

- **What do you bring to the world?** What is that special thing about you that you want to share with others, that thing that's going to "influence" them? If you love something, is it something that others will love, too?

Do you believe in what you offer? This might sound silly, but if you don't believe in yourself and what you can do as an influencer, no one else will, either.

What sets you apart from other influencers in your group? What makes you unique?

If you don't believe in yourself and what you can do as an influencer, no one else will, either.

You can always learn more, of course, but start with what you do know.

So don't just go into it with the idea that you'll figure out something later. Start with something solid at the start. And forget about pretending to be into something, just to try to get famous; people can spot a phony a mile away!

- **Do you understand what you're offering?** If you want to be a clothing influencer, you'd better already have some knowledge about the kinds of clothes you like! You can always learn more, of course, but start with what you do know.

- **Will others believe in what you have to offer?** Now that you know what it is you want to bring to the world, ask yourself if it's what others really need. It may be cool to you, but if you can't convince others that it is, too, you're not going to get very far.

- **Why should people follow you?** What is it about you that should make people want to give you their

Who are the people most likely to connect with you and your unique message?

time, get invested in you, and keep up with your stories? Basically, what's in it for them?

- **Who should follow you?** Who are the people most likely to connect with you and your unique message? And don't just say "everyone." Nobody appeals to everyone; sorry, but it's true! In fact, the more you can drill down to exactly the kinds of people you want following you, the better your chances of attracting genuine followers.

- **Are you relatable?** This question pairs with the one above. Are you someone that can reach others and make them feel like they know you, or want to? You might not be sure yet, or you might think you can't do this, when you actually can. Also, remember that your online persona will be different than what people see in real life.

Are you someone that can reach others and make them feel like they know you, or want to?

- **What is your voice?** Is it totally casual? Is it more professional? Is it educational? Knowing what kind of tone you have will make a difference in what you're offering and who will follow you. Again, don't try to be everything to everyone. You can always shift it later if it's not working, but for now, pick a style and stick with it.

- **Is your brand something that works across lots of social media platforms, or is it better only on one or two?** Consider where your work will be best used. If one platform is better than another, focus on that one at first, and don't waste valuable time somewhere else. You might be able to expand as you gain followers and influence. It's probably best to start small, even with just one platform at first.

- **Related to that, do you have a "look" that works across platforms?** It could be a logo, a username, anything that identifies you (see "Themes and

Visual Style" below). It's not absolutely essential, but it is a good way of being recognizable in more than one place.

- **Are you willing to try new things?** Not every post you make or message you send is going to resonate with people. You'll have good ones and bad ones. Are you committed to finding the right message?

- **Is it worth partnering with another influencer in the same area?** Someone else has probably already gotten there before you, but it might be that you can team up with them, at least at first. Don't just expect this, though, and ask nicely.

Not every post you make or message you send is going to resonate with people. You'll have good ones and bad ones. Keep going.

THEMES AND VISUAL STYLE

A great way for you to stand out and make a splash is to have a recognizable style across social media platforms and your website. This doesn't need to be some elaborate design, or mean that you have to get someone to create a logo for you (though you can, if you want to!); it just means that the visuals, language, and tone of each page should be similar. It's a way of identifying you and your brand, your message, etc.

Followers will come to associate your style with you, which gives you a stronger presence and puts you ahead of the competition.

Followers will come to associate your style with you, which gives you a stronger presence and puts you ahead of the competition. Here are some ideas about how to do it:

- **Take a look at the social media sites that you use.** How are your pages similar? How are they different? You probably don't need to be on every one, at least not right away. But each will have its own design and features. What can you do to mark yourself out on each of them?

- **What styles do you like?** Think about things like colors and appearance. Are you trying to look classic? Contemporary? When you get an idea of the visual style, see how you can put it into every site you're on. Ask a friend who knows about design to help you get started. It could even be a great way to partner with a designer or artist, and help each other out.

- **Consider using the same profile photo across platforms.** This isn't required, but at first, it might make you easier to find and more identifiable. If you have a really good one, put it up on each site to help stand out. Later, as you get better known, you can think about switching to different photos for each site.

- **Think about your language.** How do you write in your posts and on your site? Are you super casual? More formal? Funny? Sarcastic? It's good to keep this tone across platforms as much as possible, because it gives you an easy way to be consistent. If you're known for being funny, for example, be funny everywhere!

- **Use a branded hashtag for your posts, if you have one** (see "The Art of the Hashtag" later on in this book). Do you have a slogan or saying, or a word that identifies you? Make sure it's on the home pages of each social media site you're on, and that it shows up in all relevant posts.

- **Think about how your users follow you.** Do you have different audiences for different platforms? You might. Even if you have a good brand or identity, some followers will prefer to follow you on one site and not the other. Some followers could love your six-minute videos on YouTube, while others might only want short TikTok videos or tweets. Think about how you can reach these different groups, but still keep your brand and look more or less the same.

- **Be ready to change it up.** Times change pretty quickly, and you have to keep up with them. So you probably don't want to keep the same theme and style forever, unless you have a really good logo or phrase. Be ready to go with the flow and change as you see your friends and competitors change.

Times change
pretty quickly,
and you have
to keep up
with them.

GAINING FOLLOWERS

Okay, so you've set up your profile(s), you've defined your niche, you've got a brand you want to present; it's all good! Now how do you gain followers, so that you're not just getting comments from your mom on how good each of your posts are? (note: moms can be great for supporting you in this, so don't ignore them!)

Many of the pieces of advice here work on several different platforms, so try them all out and see what works for you. Here are some ways to start getting those needed followers:

Before anything else, start with who you know. Tell your friends that you're starting up a new business/influencer page or pages, and ask them to follow you. Ask them to invite their friends as well. You might be surprised at how many followers you get right at the start!

Instagram

- Make sure your bio page is strong, and the link is to something really good. That might be your website, but it might be something else, and you might change it pretty often, depending on what you're posting.

- Post regularly, if not every day, then on the same days each week, and at the same times, if you can.

- Be sure to post videos; they get the most engagement. But be careful about just recycling videos from other platforms, or sharing them via links. Instagram likes you to post original content.

- Post stories. They only last for twenty-four hours, but they appear at the tops of users' feeds, so there is a better chance of them being seen. Use hashtags and location tags to let those who don't follow you see you.

- Use hashtags that are specific to your post, see "The Art of the Hashtag."

- Engage with your followers and ask them to tell their friends about you. Word of mouth and personal recommendations are still great ways of getting noticed!

- Be a bit careful with Instagram engagement groups. You may have heard about them; they try to beat Instagram algorithms, and you can join them via

Word of mouth and personal recommendations are still great ways of getting noticed!

Make sure
your content
matches what
your ideal
followers want
to see.

several other sites. They can be useful for trying to gain new followers, but you can't just go into one and expect people to follow you without following them back. Also, people have gotten in trouble or even banned by Instagram because of using them.

TikTok

- Make sure your content matches what your ideal followers want to see. Once you know who you'll be posting for, you'll have a better idea of how to zero in on those people and create engaging content.

- A lot of your potential followers will also be on Instagram, so make sure to let them know what you're doing on TikTok

- Keep up with trends on TikTok. See how they change and look for ways that you might fit with a given trend. Is there something popular that relates to what you're offering? Then get in on it! Use the right hashtags and get noticed. When people are excited for something, it increases your chances of being seen.

- Try to post when your followers are most active. You can learn about this with a pro account, which is well worth having.

- Promote your TikTok account on other social media platforms that you're on, and share your videos on them. The more people you can reach, the better!

- Try to get followers to post their own user-generated content (UGC) related to you. For example, if you give makeup tips, ask for followers to create videos using those tips, and link back to you. You can do the same for other influencers and help each other out!

Is there something popular that relates to what you're offering? Then get in on it!

- Partner up. As always, find others who are posting similar things and try a co-promotion for both of you.

- Include a call-to-action in your videos. A CTA can bring in more people, even if it's just "Follow me for more great videos like this."

Twitter

- Make your profile page appealing. As always, do something that draws viewers in and make the link a good one. You can change it as often as you want.

- Tweet often. Twitter can feel like shouting into a storm, but the more you do it, the better your chances of getting noticed. Some sites recommend that you tweet up to seven times a day, if you can. It's a numbers game, so keep at it!

- Post more tweets with images. Plain text tweets don't attract people nearly as well, unless the poster is already super famous. The more you can do to attract attention, the better. Think images, GIFs, videos, etc.

- If you retweet something (and you should!), comment on it. Explain why you're retweeting it to your followers.

- Use hashtags, but not too many. Twitter allows you to use hashtags, but don't go overboard. Two or three is enough if you make them specific. "The Art of the Hashtag" for more info.

- Take then time to reply to others you follow, if you like them and want to get noticed by their followers. It doesn't always work, but it's just possible that others will see you, if you post early enough so that you don't get lost in the many replies.

YouTube:

- When you end your videos, ask viewers to like and subscribe. It's really that simple. Everybody does it, because it works. Invite them to view more content and be sincere about it.

- If your goal is to make money using YouTube, you have to have a minimum number of subscribers. You have to have at least 1,000 subscribers to become a YouTube partner and earn ad revenue, for example.

- When you end a video, mention what you'll be posting next. Give viewers a little teaser to get them interested. That means you'll need to know what you're posting next, of course!

- Get a good camera and background. Many cell phones take awesome video, so this doesn't need to be expensive. But make sure your background looks good (even if it's just your living room), and make sure the sound is good.

- Create attractive thumbnails for your videos, and make them consistent. It's about building a brand look, so decide what that should be. You can always change it later, but your video thumbnails should look like they all came from the same source.

- Embed your videos elsewhere, such as in your website or blog. You'll get more people clicking to them that way.

- Can your videos be turned into a good playlist? Think about doing it to encourage people to watch more than one.

- Release your videos on the same days and at the same times, if you can. This will make you reliable, and people will know when they can tune in.

- Offer a reward when you hit a certain number of subscribers. This will encourage people to subscribe. Or make it very specific like, "the 2,000th subscriber will win..." New people will want to be that subscriber!

- Cross promote your videos on your other social media platforms. Of course!

- Choose your keywords carefully. Like hashtags, they will determine how you come up in searches. Take the time to learn a bit more about doing this.

- Partner with other channels and with other influencers. Again, partnering can only help you.

KNOW YOUR AUDIENCE

One of the most important things you need to do is figure out who your talking to. Who are you trying to reach, and what influence do you want to have on them? As we've mentioned, you can't just assume that you're an influencer for "everybody." Trust us, you're not, nobody is. The more you can decide on the perfect audience for you, the better your chances of being able to connect with them, interest them, and gain followers who want to know what you're all about. The smaller you make your audience at the start, the better. Here are some ideas.

Who are you trying to reach, and what influence do you want to have on them?

The more you can decide on the perfect audience for you, the better your chances of being able to connect with them, interest them, and gain followers who want to know what you're all about.

- **Think about your followers.** Who will they be? What groups are they from? What do they want from you? Why do they want it? How can you give it to them? How often do they want to hear from you? Who else do they follow? Is that person a competitor or a friend?

- **Think about who won't follow you.** Yes, this is important, because it keeps you from wasting time on people who won't follow you no matter what you do. If you know that your brand doesn't appeal to some (say, people over thirty, or anyone not in college), don't bother trying to "collect" them. You'll save yourself time and frustration!

- **If you're into math and statistics (yeah, we know!) you can look at the analytics on social media sites.** They will tell you, in the form of data, who is clicking what and when. This can be a good way to learn about who might be interested in you. But it might also be pretty boring.

- **Look at others who are influencers in the same area as you.** Why are they doing? How are they attracting followers? If they're your friends, they can probably help you grow your own following. If you don't know them, or they're competing with you, it's still worth following them and seeing how they interact with their fans and people. How is your influence different? Can you attract some of those same people?

- **Remember that not everyone will like you or care about what you do, and that's okay.** Even the biggest influencers have tons of people who can't stand them! Learning to be okay with that is a sign that you are growing in your role and can take the good with the bad. Not everyone will like you, and some people might say unkind things. But you're brave for putting yourself out there to begin with, so take heart and remember that there will always be people who want to hear what you have to say.

- **Keep up with trends.** What you're offering may be hot this year, but not next year. Remember that people can get pretty bored pretty fast, so to keep followers, you're going to have to keep them interested. And yes, that can be hard!

PERFECTING YOUR CONTENT: CAPTION WRITING, VIDEO EDITING, AND PHOTO TIPS

Captions

It's important to know what to write in your video captions, tweets, and other posts. While different platforms have different expectations, there are some good guides that work for all of them:

- **Write to your audience.** Know their language and what they expect from you. Look at other influencers in your area, and see how they post and interact.

- **Keep posts short and to the point.** Twitter limits the length of your tweets, but some other sites will let you write as much as you want. This is usually not a good idea.

- **Make your captions about your post: the photo, the video, etc.** This may seem obvious, but the more you can tie the two together, the better. If you post random text that has little or nothing to do with your visuals, who is going to make the connection? And why should they care?

- **Put the important stuff first.** Any keywords and material directly related to the photo or video should be at the beginning.

- **Make it funny.** People are much more likely to engage with your post if you can make them laugh, even a little.

- **Ask a question.** If you can get people interested in answering in the comments, you have them hooked!

- **Include a call to action.** Invite your followers to click a link to learn more, to comment, to share with their friends, etc.

- **Use hashtags at the end of your caption.** Don't put them first. This is distracting and can cause readers to tune out.

Video Editing

Knowing how to present a video is important, no matter what platform you're on. If you're focusing on YouTube, then you definitely want to get used to putting together videos, no matter how long they are.

YouTube rules the internet for video. For anything longer than sixty seconds, you're going to want to put it on YouTube. Depending on how complex your video will be, you can use YouTube's own editor, or you might need something more advanced, like Adobe Premiere Elements, or Final Cut Pro. Here are some tips about editing your content:

- **Trim it down.** Don't make it too long, and make your intros and exits quick and easy. Think about who's watching it. Do they really want to sit through a ten-minute video, or could you say everything you need to say in four minutes?

- **Change shots and angles.** If you can help it, don't just look into the camera straight on for the entire video. Try editing in shots of you at different angles. At the very least, edit in some images or other footage to break it up, even if it's just in a window next to you while you're speaking. The more dynamic you can make your video, the better.

- **Think about getting a separate microphone.** You might be able to rely on the one on your camera or phone, but a better one is probably worth investing a little money in, when you can. Even it's just one you can plug into your camera, you'll get a better sound.

- **Try to have a beginning, middle, and end.** In other words, know where you're going. You may want to write out a simple script. The more you can plan it out ahead of time, the less likely you are to ramble on and get boring!

- **Back up your videos!** There's nothing worse than losing a project you've spent hours working on because of some technical glitch. Whether it's a thumb drive, a plug-in drive, or the Cloud, make sure your videos are always stored in at least two places. Also, save your work often. You never know what might happen!

- **Check out online videos for more tips.** There are literally thousands of videos out there on how to make better videos. Start watching them!

Instagram has become increasingly good for videos, whether in regular posts or in stories. Knowing how to optimize your IG videos is essential. Here are some tips:

- **Many of the points for YouTube videos can work for Instagram, too.** So use them.

- **Post videos with the idea of keeping a similar look to them.** This doesn't mean that they all have to be shot in the same place (they shouldn't), but try to keep a style to them, something that defines you and your brand. With that in mind...

- **Look at video software for filters and effects.** There are tons of apps out there that allow you to add filters, color, and other layers. While you don't want to overuse effects (they can start to look cheap), a nice color filter on every video might be a good way to give your videos brand recognition, no matter where you shoot them.

- **Keep them short and think of what your audience wants.** What do they want and need to see from you? What's going to keep them engaged? What won't? Keep the video focused on one topic only; you can always shoot another video for a different topic!
- **Make your videos about your message.** Keep them on topic. The occasional "for fun" post is fine, but realize that you're trying to gain followers who look to you for advice and/or insight, so don't fill up their timelines with useless "fun" videos that they don't want and won't watch, anyway.

TikTok has its own built-in video editor, which is a great place to start. There are a number of great tutorials online to help you get started (with more being added all the time as people come up with new tips), but it's pretty easy, once you get the hang of it. As you get more used to editing, you might want to check out some of the other apps and program that will help you create videos.

- Much of the advice for YouTube and Instagram above applies to TikTok, as well.

You should also remember that if you are using more than one site (or all three of these or more), you should try to be consistent across platforms with your look and your message.

Photo Tips

Photos are everywhere on social media. From Facebook to Twitter to Instagram, photos still rule and you can make quite an impression with good ones. Here are some helpful tips for doing social media picture right:

- **Take a good picture to begin with.** Don't just rely on fixing it up after you've taken the shot. It's better to try to get it right first, and then make it a little better when you edit it. The old phrase "garbage in, garbage out" applies here. Don't make more work for yourself.

- **Keep your lens clean.** Whether it's a cell phone or a professional camera, make sure the lens doesn't get smudged, or your perfect photo won't be!

- **Make sure you have good lighting.** A grainy photo isn't going to do you any good. Play around a bit with your lighting to see what works best. Outside, you'll have fewer choices, but you can still try to put your subject in the best light, especially if it's you!

- **Take many photos.** You'll get a better sense of what's good and what isn't if you try them in different settings, at different angles, etc. You might even develop your own personal style out of this.

- **Don't always shoot close-ups, especially of yourself.** You may be the influencer, but give some space to your surroundings. If you're in front of a cool building, on the side of a mountain, etc., make sure to make that the main focus of your shot.

- **Play around with editing software.** There are countless different editing apps out there. Give a few a try and see which one works for you. But as with video, be careful about overdoing it with filters and/or effects. Once in a while is fine, but they can make your shots look tacky if you overdo them, and boring if you always use the same one.

- **Make your photos match your captions.** Tell a story with your picture, one that aligns with your message.

- **Make sure your resolution and size/shape are correct for the platform you're using.** There are ideal sizes for photos, so make sure you know which are which, depending on the social media site you're posting them to. They'll look better and save you the embarrassment of posting something that doesn't fit, or gets cut off!

THE ART OF THE HASHTAG

Some platforms, especially Instagram, rely on hashtags. You likely already know what they are, but here is a quick refresher and some ideas on how to use them to help boost your visibility. Let's start by answering a few basic questions:

- **What are hashtags?** Hashtags are words, or combinations of letters, numbers, or even emojis that are preceded by the pound (#) sign. They are used to identify the content of your post and make it easier for users to find when they search for those keywords.

- **Why use them?** Because if you do, they will appear on a page of search results for that keyword or symbol. So if you use a hashtag like #redhair, everyone who searches for "redhair" will have a chance of seeing your post when it comes up in the search results. People will even follow certain hashtags, so that they can be notified whenever someone posts new content that uses that particular tag. Twitter also posts trending hashtags on people's home pages.

- **Why do people like them?** Because if it's something they are interested in, they want to see all the related posts about it. It's a way of marking our posts so that they can be found by exactly the people that want to see them.

So, now that we've answered those questions, how can you use hashtags to your advantage?

- **Make sure your hashtags are related to your post.** Just putting in random, popular ones will do you no good. You want to make sure that they are a part of your follower's interests, and specific to your post.

- **Be careful how many you use.** On Twitter, it's best to limit the number to no more than two or three. On Instagram, you can use a lot more, but even there, no more than ten should be enough to get your message across and make your post easier to find.

- **Make your hashtags short.** You want your tags to be easily searchable, and things that people will likely look up. Use tags like #ussoccer and #hairspray, not tags like #pizzaisthebestfoodinthewolrdomgitsamazing... you get the idea!

- **Make them easy to think of and remember.** If you use something like a different spelling for a common word, or a mixture of different emojis, how many people will actually think to look that up?

- **At the same time, don't make them too common.** If your hashtag is just #eyemakeup, there are going to be thousands of posts for this term! But if you can make it a bit more unique, like #glittereyeshadow, or #glittermakeup, this might cut down the competition. Yes, trying to keep it simple, but also unusual enough to stand out is hard!

- **Not every post needs a hashtag.** Use them when you're really trying to make a statement, or draw attention to something about your brand. It's okay for some posts not to have them.

- **Look at other people's hashtags.** Look at influencers who are in the same area as you. What hashtags are they using? Is there anything there that could be useful for you to use, too?

- **Use a saying or brand identifier.** Is there a word or a phrase that you like to use to identify yourself? This is a great one for a hashtag. Maybe your brand has a slogan, like "Nailed it" for your topic, nails and nail polish. So a hashtag like #nailedit is great to use in every post where you talk about this.

- **For Instagram, use hashtags for posts and for stories.** You can't use as many on a story, but it's still a good idea to include them.

- **Be careful about banned hashtags.** It's unlikely, but check to make sure you're not using any hashtags that aren't allowed on the site. Often, these are spam or scam hashtags. Also avoid things like #follow me, or #ifollowback, etc.

- **Use different hashtags on different posts.** If you use the exact same ones for every post, you will show up less in feeds and searches.

- **Create a list of your favorites.** Just because you don't want to use them in every post doesn't mean you shouldn't keep track of your favorites. It'll be easier to remember them that way.

DIGITAL MARKETING

Marketing is everything, and these days, so much of it is done online. You might think of marketing as advertising, spending money on ads, or maybe hiring people to promote you, but there's so much more to it than that, and you don't have to spend a lot of money. Before we go too much further, it's good to know what kinds of marketing there are:

- **Content marketing:** This kind of marketing is where you offer something useful to your followers. It establishes you as an authority, and you don't ask for anything in return; you're not selling anything, you're giving something away. A good example: let's say you're into hair care and products. Maybe three times a week, you release a short video with a hair care tip. You give this information away, and you can ask followers to comment on what they'd like to see in future videos.

- **Affiliate marketing:** This kind of marketing is best if you have a product. You get others to advertise your product or service, and when they buy it, the person who advertises it gets a small cut of the money, that way, you both win! Because if they bring in new customers for you, you don't have to do the work, and they make a bit of money. Unless you're selling something, you probably won't use this kind of marketing.

- **Newsletter and blogs:** If you like writing, these can be great ways to keep in touch with your followers. If you're not so big on writing, consider doing a video or audio instead. Having a list of people who want to receive what you send out is a great thing, and will help get you established as the influencer you want to be. You don't have to write long posts; in fact, people prefer if you don't. But you can use them again as places to give value to your followers. Send out links to your new YouTube videos, for example. If you want people to sign up for a mailing list or a blog notification, offer them something in exchange, a secret video, or a tip sheet on a pdf, etc. Make sure that you let people know about your list or blog on your social media platforms.

- **Teaming up with other influencers:** Are there other influencers you like and want to work with? Try teaming up and advertising each other's platforms, websites, etc. You'll both get exposure to new followers and may pick up quite a few that way! If you have a friend who sells something, why not advertise it for them? If you have something you want them to promote, ask them! You can help each other grow. You may eventually have a whole network of other influencers that you can go to over and over, and they can come to you. People often follow several influencers in one area, so help each other.

- **Search Engine Optimization (SEO):** SEO is a big thing right now, and if you have a website, you need to understand it, at least a little. Basically, it means making sure that a search engine finds your site first, or at least in the top few results. It's too big a topic to go into here, but take the time to learn a little about it, or ask someone who knows all about it. Everyone wants to be noticed and turn up first in search results, so in order to do that, you're going to have to get into SEO, at least a little.

- **Paid advertising:** This is probably something you'll want to avoid, at least at first. While it can make a difference in getting your message out, especially to established businesses, it also can be a huge waste of money. And if you have only a little money, you don't want to waste it! The only time it might be worth doing is when you pay a small amount of money to a social media site to "boost" a post once in a while. You'll definitely get it seen by more people that way, but is it worth it? You can try it once, spend $5 or $10, and see how it goes. But remember a lot of people hate ads, and if a post says that it's a "sponsored post," a lot of people will just ignore it.

- **Podcasts and webinars:** Check out "Getting Known with Podcasts and Webinars" for more info on how to make use of these great online tools!

Taking Advantage of your Website

If you have a website (and you probably should!), there are many ways of using it that will help get your name and brand out there. Here are some tips for making it stand out:

- **Make sure it looks good.** You can do it yourself, or have someone design it for you, but make sure that it's up-to-date (unless you're going for a deliberately retro look), and has all the features that modern users are looking for. It has to be easy to navigate. It needs to reflect your brand and your personality, and only you can decide how it will look, though a designer can help if you need it.

- **SEO (again!).** Get help with this, if you need it. Good SEO will get you in the top rankings of an internet search!

- **Make sure you update it regularly.** Have you seen those websites that haven't been updated in a year or two? Yeah, who cares about those? Why would your followers want to visit if you don't have anything new for them?

- **Give something away.** A secret video, a pdf, something. Let people have it in exchange for signing up for your mailing list. You gain followers; they get something that not everyone has.

- **Make a few pages easily sharable on social media and other places.** Make it easy for your followers to let their friends know about you by having "Share on" buttons and links at the bottom of blogs, news, video pages, etc.

- **Make your site easy to use, and full of value.** Don't let people get lost or wonder why they're even there.

- **If you're comfortable with the idea, make it easy for people to contact you.** Contact forms are pretty normal on a lot of websites, but it's up to you how contactable you want to be. If you're under eighteen, there could be legal and safety issues to think about. If you don't accept DMs on social media sites, then you may not want a contact form on your website, and that's fine.

HOW TO STAND OUT FROM THE CROWD

As an influencer, it's important that you are as unique as possible. People have to see that you're special and can give them something that others can't. That sounds great, but how do you do that?

- **Always try to grow your following.** You may get 100, 500, or 1,000 followers at the start, and that's great! But what if you could get 10,000? Keep in touch with your regular followers and ask them to recommend you to others. If you're offering great content, your brand will sell itself when their friends see what you do. Related to that...

- **Let your followers do the work for you.** If you're offering great things to them, they're going to be enthusiastic and want to tell others about you. But the catch is that you have to provide the good content, constantly. If you do, your influence can grow organically. "Word of mouth" is still a great way to spread news, even in the digital age!

Make everything you do have value.

- **Be careful not to try to grow too quickly.** You might daydream about going viral and being an overnight sensation, and that's great, but think about what happens after that: can you keep up with thousands of new followers? Can you provide enough content to keep them engaged? If you're just doing this in your spare time, do you have enough time to be able to do more if you need to? It's easy to get overwhelmed if you go viral, so be careful. You could be a victim of your own success!

- **Always be thinking about adding new content, but don't overwhelm your followers.** Make everything you do have value, even if you post multiple times a day. People are already hit with thousands of new bits of information every day, so keep them engaged with valuable content.

- **Consider partnering with other influencers.** If someone has a bigger following than you and likes what you do, ask if you can partner on some posts, or messages. You'll be shown to their audience and might gain followers. Just be careful that you're not using others for this purpose. Be genuine and try to offer them something in return. See "Working with Brands and Getting Sponsors" below to get other ideas on partnering.

- **As always, watch what others are doing in your field, both friends and competitors.** How are they standing out? What could you do differently or better? What are you not doing that they're doing?

Be genuine.

WORKING WITH BRANDS AND GETTING SPONSORS

Getting sponsors is a great way to increase your visibility online and get your brand recognized. And it doesn't just have to be online, there are lots of ways to connect and use sponsorship to help you. If someone wants you to sell their brand, you can partner with them, so that you both benefit. They'll get the advertising they want,

and you'll get a much wider audience to see you and
who you are.

- **Try reaching out to a company you like to see if
they ever work with influencers and media person-
alities.** There's a good chance they do, if it can help
them sell more of their product or service!

- **Start small, unless you think you can get Coca
Cola's attention right away!** Honestly, you probably
won't. Find out who runs the company's marketing
and advertising and try to have a talk with them.

- **You can advertise a product that you like or believe
in on your social media platforms:** in photos, videos,
posts, etc.

- **You might get paid by the company for agreeing to
advertise for them, which is great!** But you will also
likely get access to their followers and their network,

a whole new group that's never have heard of you. Doing things for "exposure" is often a bad idea, but in this case, it just might work.

- **Even if a company doesn't have a lot of money or a big following, it might be worth partnering with them.** This is especially true if they have a product that relates to who you are, or a following that you'd like to tap into.

- **You can partner with a sponsor at an event (like a convention for a fandom, a music genre, etc.), a concert, an outdoor festival that you like, etc.** Basically, try anywhere that you can increase your visibility and gain followers.

- **Start out locally and go from there.** There are probably a lot of potential sponsors and events in your area that are good prospects, even if you're not super famous yet.

- **Consider working with a charity that you believe in.** Agree to make an appearance at one of their events. You won't get paid, but you'll be visible, and working for something you like. It's really good social proof that you stand behind your message. You don't always need the message to be just about you.

- **Make sure that you choose events and sponsors that are followed by the kind of people you want to reach.** It doesn't really do you any good to try to get money from a hardware store if you don't have any interest in what they're doing! If you're into clothing, don't look for sponsorship by a computer company, unless there's an obvious connection.

- **Make sure that any sponsors or events that you do work with are the real deal.** There are a lot of scams out there, and you don't want your good name associated with them! Do some background checking, and make sure they are honest and on the level.

So why go to the trouble of doing all this?

- **You can advertise your connection or event across all your platforms, and get your sponsor/partner to do the same thing.** That increases your potential audience, especially if they are bigger than you are!

- **It makes you stand out.** As an influencer, you need to be doing things that others aren't. Getting out into the real world and not just being online is a great way to show that you're a real person and not just a made-up personality.

- **It's social proof.** If a company trusts you to advertise their product, or to deliver their message, it means you're someone worthy of attention. That makes you more appealing to potential new followers.

- **It lets you get to know loads of people you didn't know before.** People that follow the other company now know about you; you've increased your audience with a fraction of the work!

- **You might gain some more partners.** If other companies, influencers, or sponsors see you and like what you do, they may want to team up with you, too! The more you can grow that network, the better!

- **If you have a good relationship with a sponsor, maybe they'll want to put out something related to you:** a tee shirt, a phone case, yoga pants, whatever. Wouldn't be cool to see your name and design on something like that?

Working with a sponsor or an advertiser is definitely worth your time!

MONETIZING YOUR PLATFORM AND NEGOTIATING YOUR WORTH

One of the great things about being better known as an influencer and someone who people trust is that you have the opportunity to monetize your platform; that's right, you can actually make money from being on social media! That's the good news. The not-so-good news is that it takes time and a lot of work, just like everything else. So how do you go about bringing in the cash? Here are some ideas:

- **Make sure you have everything in place.** Look professional, be consistent, have a brand that stands out, and be trustworthy. If you're going to attract potential investors, you have to show them that you're serious about being an influencer.

- **You'll need to have a following.** Unless you're lucky, you won't be as likely to monetize your online presence at first. It's going to take some time. You need to build up a group of followers, and get your name out there as a trusted expert in your niche; social proof is everything. That doesn't mean you need to have a million followers before you can start; far from it. But you need it be looking at thousands of followers, not hundreds. Do you have, 8,000? 5,000? Even 3,000? You can probably start thinking about it.

Look professional,
be consistent,
have a brand that
stands out, and be
trustworthy.

- **Offer products for sale.** Are you interested in selling something, anything from artwork to beauty products? You need to get the message out online and on your platforms. It may be something you make yourself, or it may be that you are already partnering with a company to sell their products (see below). In that case, you endorse the product and offer a link to buy it, and when people use that specific link to buy, you get a small payment for each click. This is usually called affiliate marketing or sales, and can be helpful when you're starting out.

- **Offer online tutorials.** Do you know a lot about a subject, any subject? Is it something you can teach to others? It might be worth looking into creating an online course, or several courses. It can be very easy to set these up nowadays, and it could be a great source of income, once you do the initial work and get them going. Your best bet is to offer some content for free, say a shorter video on YouTube, or some teasers on TikTok, and then leave a link to where interested viewers can learn more and sign up for the whole video class.

- **Partner with businesses.** This can be one of the best ways to make money. After you have a good enough reputation, you might find businesses coming to you to endorse their products. That's when you know you've "made it" as an influencer, because that company is telling you that your endorsement will "influence" their customers to buy. And once you've done a few of these, more will probably keep coming!

- **Reach out to smaller businesses.** If businesses aren't coming to you yet, try reaching out to them instead. Start small and work up. Is there a local company that would like some help? You might want to offer to advertise their products or services for free at first, because it will be helping you get better known, too. Then after you've done a few of these, you have a small portfolio of endorsements that you can show to other businesses.

- **Go to events.** Events have been curtailed during the pandemic, but they will come roaring back soon enough. It's worth your time to try to go to events and conventions that are related to your area of influence, not only to meet others who are interested, but as a possible place for sales. If you're selling something, maybe consider having a small booth where people can stop by and chat with you, learn about you and sign up to follow you. The in-person, human connection still goes a long way!

- **Consider ad revenue.** YouTube offers channels with large enough view numbers and subscribers the chance to monetize their videos with ads. Not everyone likes doing this, and yes, most people hate ads in their videos, but it might be worth considering, if you have a lot of YouTube subscribers. Do some research on monetizing your YouTube videos and see if it's right for you. Many YouTube channels do make a good amount of money.

Negotiating

Okay, so you've been approached by a company or brand that would like your endorsement. Awesome! But now what? How do you negotiate with them to make sure that you receive what you deserve and they get what they want?

- **Ask yourself what you would like out of this partnership.** What's in it for you? Sure, it would be nice to get your face out there more, but can there be more to it than that? Could this be an ongoing partnership, or is it just a one-time thing? Is the money what you really want, or is getting bet-ter-known just as important?

- **Ask them what their budget is.** This is fine to do if they haven't given you a number yet. It's import-ant to know what they're working with, so you can decide whether or not it's for you. A smaller com-pany will have a smaller budget, and that's fine when you're starting out. Again, you're getting experience and social proof, so don't say no to a low offer, if they seem like good people and really want to part-ner with you; don't get greedy!

- **Find out about the business.** Check out their website, see what they do, and see what they need. Are they a legitimate, ethical company? Have they worked with other influencers before? How did that go? What will they do with your endorsement?

- **Ask your friends and colleagues.** If you get an offer, ask one of your influencer friends what they think. How much would they charge? Is the offer fair? Does it seem sketchy?

- **It's okay to negotiate.** It's not rude (unless you act rude doing it!). Find out what they really expect of you, and what they're okay with you doing. Are there things they can offer you in addition to money, such as product, a chance to be a guest on their blog or video, etc.? It might be that they can give you some legit exposure that will really help you, too. But don't do the whole thing for "exposure," unless you really like the company and think partnering with them will help you.

- **If they've come to you, they should pay you something.** They should realize your value as an influencer and be prepared to pay you for that. If they ask you to pay them, run away! It's a scam and a waste of your time. You should never pay to endorse anything!

- **How much is enough?** It really depends on what you'll be doing for them. There are no hard and fast rules here. You might want to check with other influencers who have done similar deals and see how it worked out for them, just to have a rough idea of what the amount should be. As you receive more endorsement offers and get used to doing them, it will be a good idea to make a rate sheet, i.e., what you charge for specific services.

Realize your value.

THE YOUNG INFLUENCER'S HANDBOOK

- **Get it in writing.** All agreements should be in writing, so that you know what's expected of you, and they have to commit to paying you for it. Read through any contracts they offer you, to make sure you aren't getting stuck in something you don't want. It's not a bad idea to have a lawyer or at least a friend with some legal knowledge look it over and make sure everything's good.

- **Keep the communication open going forward.** If you do one endorsement for a business, and they like it, they may well come back for more, which is a great thing! They might even recommend you to other companies. Always keep those doors open.

FINAL THOUGHTS

There's never been a better time to be an influencer. With millions upon millions of people online every second of every day, you have the chance to reach untold numbers of people, people who want to hear your message, interact with you, see your brand, buy your products and services, and take your advice. You can also get completely lost in the noise of so many people shouting over each other for attention!

This little book will get you started, but it's really just the beginning. Do more research online. Read everything you can about influencers, especially in areas where you want to influence, too.

You have the
chance to reach
untold numbers of
people, people who
want to hear your
message, interact
with you, see
your brand, buy
your products and
services, and take
your advice.

You'll never "arrive," it will just be a stop on a longer trip that you'll keep taking for as long as you want to be an influencer.

Part of being an influencer is about being up on the latest trends. New apps, new programs, new ideas, and new tips are showing up all the time. New social media platforms come around, while some established ones go away. Even the mighty sites like Twitter and Instagram probably won't be here forever, so always be looking for the next big thing. Never stop learning and growing.

If you want to position yourself as an expert, you'll need to keep working at it. You'll never "arrive," it will just be a stop on a longer trip that you'll keep taking for as long as you want to be an influencer. But that's a big part of the fun of it all.

Good luck with your influencer journey!

ABOUT APPLESAUCE PRESS

Good ideas ripen with time. From seed to harvest, Applesauce Press crafts books with beautiful designs, creative formats, and kid-friendly information on a variety of fascinating topics. Like our parent company, Cider Mill Press Book Publishers, our press bears fruit twice a year, publishing a new crop of titles each spring and fall.

Visit us online at
cidermillpress.com

or write to us at
PO Box 454
12 Spring Street
Kennebunkport, Maine 04046